Good Winter

*A Smallish Guide
to Making the Most
of a Bleak Season*

DYLAN HIGGINS

ISBN:1983582913
ISBN-13:978-1983582912

CONTENTS

TO BEGIN

Christmas ends. All the festive gatherings and outings cease. We take down the stockings and ornaments and remove the trees. Suddenly, our home seems bleak in contrast to the celebratory month that has just passed. A glance out the window reveals that the yard is just as stark. Somehow in the midst of decking the halls we might not have taken the time to see the last leaves drifting down from their heights. All is stripped to the bare bone now. Perhaps without realizing it, the Winter Solstice slipped by too and now winter has truly set in.

Much of the world views winter as an adversary, and for good reasons. Just as spring is akin to new life, so winter is related to death. In the winter of 1609-1610, the settlers of the newly formed Virginia colony were met by a winter that truly brought death. This particular winter came to be known as The Starving Time, one in which three-quarters of the English colonists died of starvation and diseases related to a lack of food. Poets have expressed a similar sentiment where winter is concerned. Renowned Scottish poet, Robert Burns, once wrote the following lines in a poem called *Winter: A Dirge*:

The wintry west extends his blast,

And hail and rain does blaw;

Or, the stormy north sends driving forth

The blinding sleet and snaw:

While tumbling brown,

the burn comes down,

And roars frae bank to brae;

And bird and beast in covert rest,

And pass the heartless day. (1)

As Burns writes, the days can seem very "heartless" in winter. Many studies show the science behind the dark moods of winter, known better as Seasonal Affective Disorder (SAD). SAD has been labeled as a form of depression brought on, in part, by lack of sunlight. Some studies have gone as far as to suggest that the suicide rate rises in the winter, while there are just as many studies to the contrary. Whatever the case, most anyone you talk to will breathe a sigh of dismay at the mention of the looming cold of the winter months. Yes, it would seem that winter carries with it many negative connotations. But this little work is not about the bad of winter. It's about the good in it.

Yes, our moods may darken and, yes, our homes and yards may seem bleak but I believe, for one, that there is much to celebrate in winter. In the pages that follow I will frame for you what winter has become and is still becoming at Hill Hårow, the Higgins family home. These are ideas and philosophies that are fast becoming a tradition for us, at a time of year devoid of lots of special observances, due in part, I believe, to the saturation of Christmas customs, freshly experienced. But it doesn't follow that just because we have experienced a season rich with tradition that we cannot enter directly into a new time of celebration. As the winter birds arrive with the new year, so too, we can arrive at new focuses and partake in new festivities that embrace the offerings of winter - a good winter.

Good Winter

OFFERING ONE: STARS

Though my soul may set in darkness, it will rise in perfect light; I have loved the stars too fondly to be fearful of the night. - Sarah Williams, 1936 (2)

The most majestic of wonders that the winter has to offer is the night sky. With less day there is inevitably more night - and quality-night, at that. The winter sky is a clearer sky. This is due in part to less humidity in the atmosphere. With less water in the air it is not as dense; further, there is less light refraction to deal with because of the lack of water droplets in the air. This, coupled with more hours of darkness, makes for the best stargazing our atmosphere has to offer. What a view it is! Some of the greatest wonders of the heavens are visible at winter in the Northern Hemisphere, which is where I live and write and view the sky. My love for astronomy (not to be confused with astrology, for you beginners) was nurtured throughout my childhood. I have an astronomer for a father who served in leadership for the *Atlanta Astronomy Club* before leaving the city to establish a new group, the *Flint River Astronomy Club*. Star gazing runs deep in my family. I grew up with a small observatory in my backyard and spent many a cold, cold night peering up with my father. So it is a delight to be able to impart a sliver of my enthusiasm to my children and to you, good reader.

Most prominent among the winter constellations is the great hunter, Orion. He is known best for his three-starred belt and nebula. Orion's Nebula is a stellar nursery located below the belt, a fuzzy star near the middle of the line of stars making up Orion's sword. This nebula can be seen with the naked eye but a pair of binoculars will bring it into better focus. If you were to draw a more or less straight line from Orion's belt to the right, straight out into the night sky you would find the Pleiades a.k.a. the Seven Sisters. The Japanese word for this constellation is Subaru - like the car company. Next time you see a Subaru take note of the logo made up of stars. The Pleiades looks like a tiny question mark in the sky and is often mistaken for Ursa Minor (the Little Dipper) because of its shape. But the Seven Sisters are a much smaller object in the sky than the Little Dipper. Nevertheless, it is a fascinating constellation to behold and one, along with Orion, that has been talked about for thousands upon thousands of years.

The earliest Biblical writing gives an account of these two stellar figures. While Genesis deals with more ancient matters, Job is the oldest written book of Bible. We know this based on the ancient Hebraic language that was used to write Job. Languages change over time. It would be easy to tell the differences between Old English and Modern English. So too there are similar distinctions found throughout ancient forms of Hebrew. Some have argued that Job might possibly be the oldest existing text in the world. Whether or not this is the case it is still important to note that one of the earliest accounts known to mankind makes mention of Orion and Pleiades. Let's take a quick look at just one of the verses that mentions the constellations. In Job 38:31, Job has questioned the Lord's decision and He asks Job in return, "Can you bind the chains of the Pleiades or loose the cords of Orion?"(3) At first glance this might not seem overly amazing. However, with the recent scientific discoveries concerning the star activity in both of these constellations one's entire outlook may change. First, astrophysicists have discovered that the Pleiades is what is known as a gravitationally bound cluster of stars. Big words that simply mean these stars are not budging in relation to one another. They are bound as if by chains! According to NASA, the Seven Sisters will not separate for hundreds of millions of years. (4) Then there is Orion. According to past studies, the stars that make up the constellation of Orion are notedly moving apart. An article published by *Astronomy Trek* also adds that the stars of Orion, "are located at such great distances from us that the constellation will remain recognizable a long time after most of the other constellations, whose stars are closer to earth, have morphed into new shapes." (5) I call attention to this fact to say that even when the other constellations have lost their form, Orion will still be known as will the Scripture concerning him. What an amazing thing to discover the scientific validity of God's own words as written down in the ancient book of Job.

Orion's hunting dogs: Canis Major and Canis Minor are overhead as well. In fact the former contains the brightest star in the night sky known by the name Sirius. (A trivial side note, it seems that J.K. Rowling was intentional about her beloved character Sirius Black having the ability to change into a dog. After all, "Canis" is Latin for "dog.")

Gemini, the twins, can also be found making their way across the wintry night sky, not to mention the real Little Dipper whose place remains fixed in the northern sky, tethered by the last star in its handle, Polaris - more commonly referred to as the North Star. Let's not forget the most obvious of night-sky objects our own Moon, who waxes and wanes several times throughout the course of winter. Thankfully, you don't have to stay up late to see the stars at this time of year. A telescope would be great, binoculars would do just fine but if you have neither it really doesn't matter. Just bundle up, grab a cup of hot cocoa and get out there! There is one thing you have to watch out for besides the stars and that's light pollution. This is a growing issue in our world today. If you live in the city or a big town then plan a few trips to the countryside. Invite some friends, make it a big to do! Oh, and you might want to download a star app like *Night Sky* to help you navigate your way around the heavens. It is helpful to cut on the red-light feature because it makes it easier for your eyes to adjust to the sky while referencing the app.

While we're still on the subject of stars it is worth noting that they play a large role in the Church's observance of Epiphany, which begins on January 6th. A part of the liturgical calendar, Epiphany focuses, in part, on the three magi who followed celestial directions from an eastern location to find the Christ child. This day is also referred to as Three Kings Day.

Something my family has recently begun doing is creating festive ornaments and wall hangings to celebrate God's twinkly creation within the comfort of our home. In other words, we like to bring the night-sky indoors for the winter. It is good to be reminded of the grandeur of the Universe while at the same time remembering that, of all God's designs, we are the ones made in His image. The Psalmist had similar thoughts:

> When I look at your heavens, the work of your fingers, the moon and the stars, which you have set in place, what is man that you are mindful of him, and the son of man that you care for him? Yet you have made him a little lower than the heavenly beings and crowned him with glory and honor. You have given him dominion over the works of your hands; you have put all things under his feet, all sheep and oxen, and also the beasts of the field, the birds of the heavens, and the fish of the sea, whatever passes along the paths of the seas. O LORD, our Lord, how majestic is your name in all the earth! (Psalm 8:3-9)

A little twine, a tree branch hung horizontally, and some homemade golden stars and moons dangling beneath go a long way. The decorations remind us of what awaits us in the brisk air when the sun goes down, if we dare to brave the cold!

Good Winter
OFFERING TWO: WARMTH

While the winter itself has little to offer by way of warmth, we humans excel at adding this necessary touch. Henry David Thoreau speaks to the necessity of warmth in his well-known work, *Walden*. In this get-back-to-the-basics memoir, Thoreau writes that, "The grand necessity, then, for our bodies, is to keep warm, to keep the vital heat in us." (6) He goes on to say that our food and clothing and beds and homes all have one end: warmth or the desired "animal heat" as Thoreau refers to it. I see his point, as I think anyone could. Here's a recent example from my own life: I woke up the day after Christmas to a heating system that decided it had had quite enough. Needless to say, it was cold! I have a wife and four children, all of whom had yet to exit the warmth of their blankets. But they would soon enough! I jumped up and my very first thought, before, *what am I going to feed the kids?* or, *what projects need completing today?* was, *how can I make it warmer in this house?* Warmth is at the core of all our human needs. If we're not warm we are in no way prepared to do good work or be good parents and certainly, we are in no position to be artistic or productive until we first meet that need of being warm.

Getting warm can take a little more effort in winter to be sure. But it is in that effort that we often come together with those that are dearest to us and huddle close in a way that the summer would never allow for. Winter causes us to get a little creative about achieving our state of warmth and that creativity brings us, often, to the kitchen to concoct hot meals in the forms of soup, chilly and stew. These are some of the most nourishing and cherished types of sustenance for the Higgins family in the deep of winter. I'd be doing myself and the reader a disservice if I did not also mention that wassail or hot apple cider is a staple in our home in winter. Many a chilly day a big pot can be found steaming on our stovetop, filled with sliced apples, oranges, and cinnamon sticks. Delicious! Not to mention the coffee, the Earl Grey, and the cocoa! These warm foods and drinks have a knack for bringing us closer together as a family.

Another thing that brings us together is the hearth. We cut our wood together and keep that fire burning much of the winter. As we gather by the fire with hands stretched toward the warmth we laugh with each other and play games. Just last week all six of us camped out on the floor, falling asleep to an audiobook, as the firelight flickered on the ceiling above. This is a part of the magic of winter time! Warmth is one of the elements of the season that make it a good winter because we are ever aware of the stark contrast between the cold and the warmth, mere centimeters from one another through a pane of glass.

At Hill Hårow we do a few small things in our home to remind us of the wintry world beyond the walls. Though we have recently taken down the Nativity and homemade stockings from the mantelpiece we are quick to redecorate the desolate shelf in a wintery theme. We do this in varying ways but a few staples are a strand of Edison Bulbs laid across the mantel with a handcrafted white-cloth wreath made by JoAlison, my wife, and Eisley, my eldest daughter. The white wreath, set on the cedar mantel reminds me of the winter world outside and makes me more thankful for the fire blazing beneath it.

It is not out of the ordinary to find an arrangement of pine cones somewhere in our home, as well as a few lanterns strategically placed. The latter decoration has multiple layers of meaning for our family. Of course, lanterns were once needed in the dark of winter and their presence in our house stands as a reminder of our blessed modern utilities but there is another reason. If you are at all familiar with my other writings you've already figured it out, perhaps. As the author of children's fictional series *The Emblem & The Lantern*, lanterns are near and dear to my heart. The series is framed by light-bearers taking a Magic Lantern into the darkness to face the unknown land beyond and to possibly help the dark-dwellers that they seek. The story reminds me much of the lights that warm the winter and even more of the light of Christ that pierces the darkness. One last thing we will add to our trimmings this year is homemade luminaries crafted with white cups, a hole puncher and tea lights. This is, perhaps, the finishing touch to our celebration of Good Winter utilizing the warmth of light.

Good Winter
OFFERING THREE: TIME TO PONDER

When the sun goes down at 5:30 pm our children inevitably go to sleep earlier than they would in the summer. This might or might not be encouraged by my wife and I but it lends to quieter evenings for us. It is really the only time of year that we get this down time, now that our kids are a little older. We know that practices and school events wait just around the bend in spring and so we are thankful for this special time.

Sometimes we spend these extra hours reading to one another or watching Netflix (we don't have regular TV). But sometimes they are just free hours for our minds to roam where ever they will. It seems that during the winter months I do much of my deepest study of Scripture, a good deal more writing, and independent learning. I write and produce a little podcast called *Ponder This.* The tagline for the show says, "*Ponder This Podcast* is a mix of theological inquiry, narrative and original music crafted to kindle wonder in the life of the believer." The ideas for these shows almost exclusively come in the winter months when I have more time to think on things deeply and find a new sense of wonder in what I study and observe. We need wonder in our lives. Someone once said, "Wonder is the desire for knowledge." I agree. Sound knowledge flows from truth and truth flows from God. Wonder can awaken sincere worship and it can birth authentic study of God's Word.

Outside of the Word, which I recommend starting with (and lingering on), the world of education is in a constant state of change. As an educator, myself, I am always following this flux. With this change comes new and in-novative ways for us to learn. One such way is the plethora of free online courses, now offered by universities around the globe. These courses are often formatted for endless amounts of participants, thus they are called Massive Open Online Courses or MOOCs for short. I have recently taken mind-stimulating courses from Harvard University and the University of Barcelona, both of which have greatly aided my understanding of the respective content areas I was studying. While free to the user, most of the schools offer official validation for completing the courses for a nominal fee. I have been able to use these certified courses as continuing education credits as a teacher. While these online classes are available year round, it is in winter that I find myself having enough time to learn something entirely new to me. MOOCs aren't the end all to learning, of course. I recently purchased a Latin primer published in the late 1800's from Amazon. I have been using the primer to learn the basics of Latin. Again, the winter seems to be the most productive time for me where learning is concerned. Perhaps it could be for you as well.

Good Winter
OFFERING FOUR: FORMATION

Many would read this chapter and, perhaps, think of New Year's resolutions. Those people would not be too far off. Formation, as I use the term, is a time of reformation for some - a thorough washing away of what they were before. For others, formation is more like a restoration - a honing in on what really matters and who we really are, though we may have forgotten momentarily. The act of formation is more than an aesthetic resolution, though it can encompass that as well. Just as the snow (or heavy frost in Georgia) comes to prepare the land for renewal and new growth, in the same way winter can be a time where we dig in, introspectively, and get to the heart of who we are. But first, we have to know what really matters to us. We have to ask a series of honest questions. *What is my current state? What shape do I want to be in? Who or what is forming me?* Again, while this sounds like I might be referring to my physical shape it is so much more. I'm thinking in terms of holistic formation, which includes my physical form, certainly, but weighs far more heavily on spiritual matters and character development. Essentially the questions being asked are *who am I and who do I want to be?*

Winter time comes with the dawning of the new year and is a natural time to consider personal formation and act upon it. I do not pretend to know my audience overly well, so what follows is a guide that I've created for myself concerning formation and because I am first a foremost a Christian, much of what follows resonates with my faith and knowing Who should be forming me and what that form should look like. I hope that it gives you a general guide to your own formation. Let me also note that this section will dominate much this work because it is so important to get this one figured out. If you are reading this in any other season go ahead and start this step now! Chances are, you will still be working through it when winter arrives.

WE ARE GOD'S INTENDED
SO INTEND TO BE FORMED BY HIM

It was the most foreign message I'd ever seen in my inbox. The Christmas holiday was over and a new semester of teaching teenagers lay before me. I had just kissed my wife and kids goodbye and gotten into my truck. Like every morning before, I pulled out my phone to check my emails before rushing off to work. There it was! A picture of a sunshine smiling at me! It was right there in my inbox. And beneath the little icon were the words, "Your inbox is empty. Please Enjoy Your Day!"

I laughed and then actually spoke to the little sunshine saying, "Ok then, I will enjoy it!"

As I drove to school I wondered how many people had ever seen that happy little sun with his happy little message. In the days that followed, I began an impromptu survey in my community. I asked people I knew if they had ever seen the message - if their inbox was ever empty. Two out of the fifty people I questioned actually had an empty email account. Two! Most of us live with a never-ending cue of emails in our inbox. How many of those emails have we actually read? How many actually matter? It's frustrating to not be able to see the ones that matter and to discern which ones to focus on.

I run the risk of sounding a little like Forrest Gump (and of showing my age) but: life is kind of like our inbox. We're doing too much. We own too much. We are frustrated, or always on the verge of it. We have cluttered our lives with so many pursuits, so many activities and so much stuff! We no longer give our all to the things that matter most. Maybe we have even lost track of what matters most.

I have been there, recently. I naturally gravitate toward new pursuits. I would like to start a radio station with well-crafted content. But at this point, I only dabble in publishing a podcast. I want to open a bed and breakfast but first I need to learn to cook. I would like to farm my land, but how and when? I would like to become a master barber, yet I can't cut hair. I'm just shy of forty and I haven't even begun to write all the books I have piling up in my brain. Not to mention the unwritten songs nestled away inside me. There's not enough time for it all and I haven't even mentioned my family's needs! I can overload my schedule, leading to a frustrated, joy stealing life - one that I did not intend for myself. What's more, the overload not only affects me but it also affects those around me. Because of this, I began a journey to simplify life one decision at a time. To pull this off I needed a game plan.

First, I needed to remember who I am. I am intended by the mind of God and molded by His own hands. I needed to remember that I am valued by the Lord. So valued and so loved that God the Father sent His only Son to pay the debt I owed but could never repay, myself. If you're new to this idea find a Bible and turn to the Gospel of John in the New Testament. John 3:16 is what I just alluded to but you should go ahead and read the whole book for good measure.

After pausing to remember the value my life held I took a moment to think about how valuable my time was. Partially for myself but primarily for the Lord. Author and lyricist, Douglas McKelvey put it this way: "If we begin with the knowledge that our days and our hours are a precious, nonrenewable resource, then that perspective has the power to shape how we will choose to spend this hour." (7)

This train of thought helped me realize that the moments of my life are intended by God.

Maybe I should be more intentional about how I spend them - about how I am being formed.

My formational journey began with a focus statement. It is designed to lead me out of a sea of distractions and toward the shore of meaningful and joyful living. Here it is:

FOCUS ON WHAT ADDS JOY

While many things in life are the cause of fleeting happiness, authentic joy is found in a relationship with God. This joy then spills over, into His gracious gifts of family and community.

GOD, FAMILY, and COMMUNITY: these three areas are my utmost sources of joy in life. You might expect such an answer from a minister and teacher, right?

But there are others focuses in my life as well. The Lord has designed us with interests that are unique to our personal architecture. You might refer to these as individual callings.

These callings in no way belittle our main call of sharing the Gospel and making disciples of Christ. Rather, individual callings can enhance how we share the Gospel.

I have narrowed my personal callings down to two focuses. They are EDUCATION and STORYTELLING. These two focuses present themselves in many different facets of my life.

What follows is not an in-depth look at my beliefs. It is an overview of why I focus on the things that I do. It is not meant to be a detailed map for you to follow. Rather it is a grouping of road signs that will lead you in the right direction. Your focus areas must be determined by you. Joyous travels, fellow pilgrims.

<u>FIVE FOCUSES</u>

FOCUS ONE: GOD

The Lord is my Maker and Sustainer. Colossians 1:17 says that Christ holds all things together. The root of all my joy stems from my salvation in Christ and the relationship He has forged with me at the Cross. He laid His life down for me so, with a thankful heart, I seek to do the same for Him. Christ comes first in all things.

I commune with God by studying and obeying His Word. I enjoy communing with God through prayer (which consists of more listening than speaking). I find joy in singing, partaking of the Lord's Supper, and serving Him.

TIPS: PAPERLESS SCRIPTURE

It's hard to beat a leather-bound Bible in your hands for studying scripture. But if you prefer paperless then there are a few good

Bible apps available. I have two that I use. The *ESV* app from *Crossway Publishing* and the *Faithlife Study Bible* app. Both are simple and clean and the latter has great study tools.

I used to be a big fan of public radio. Over time I grew tired of the secular bent and I listen increasingly less now. I bought an audio version of the Bible and now I'm listening to the Word in my car. There is something refreshing about listening to someone read the Bible. Little things stand out in a way that they don't when I'm reading to myself. "It's like these Words were supposed to spoken," said Dylan sarcastically. But really, in all seriousness, this practice has added great value to my time with God.

FOCUS TWO: FAMILY

I was listening to talk radio one Saturday afternoon. The show featured several psychologists discussing the results of a study on family dynamics. The research determined that couples with children are less happy than couples without. The specialists went on and on about how they agreed with the study. They even answered calls from several parents who agreed wholeheartedly. Selfishness!

Why would I expect more? The world applauds selfishness as was the case with the program I was listening to. This is one reason why I don't listen to public radio very often anymore. We are born egocentric and it can get worse as we grow up. We should pray for mindsets like this to be changed by Christ. For more on why we should not be selfish, I offer these transcripts from one of my podcasts:

PONDER THIS: EPISODE FOUR

IMAGE-BEARERS

Approximately 7 billion people live on Earth today - each of us, young in the grand scheme of things. After all, there are in the neighbor-hood of 6,500 years worth of recorded history and even the oldest living among us represent a meager century in time.

So here we are - billions of children - trying to make sense of this thing called life. We do this together. We collect the past knowledge of mankind - each generation's contribution to philosophy, art, science, mathematics and religion - and we add to it.

As an interesting side note, it's easy to perceive the ancient teachers as being still among us - as if they have somehow defeated death. I have a bust of Aristotle at home. Even this father of western civilization was really no more than a blip on the radar of time. Other philosophers have added to his ideas, just as Aristotle adapted the thoughts of great thinkers before him. While Aristotelian logic lives on with us, Aristotle does not. Only a trace of him survives in his writings. The point is, we're all mere babes in the cosmos, playing our part in the ongoing story of humanity. Or is it our story at all?

Why are we here? We've all asked this question. And without trying to sound like a child in Sunday school, The Bible has the answer to our question. We were made to be image-bearers of the Creator (Genesis 1:26-27). Image-bearers, praising the Maker. This is no mundane title, no menial task - the Father's children made in His image. But are we bearing God's image properly? Judging by the course of human events I'd say we haven't always put forth our best effort.

Where did we go wrong? In Eden - where the serpent tricked our first kindred into bearing another image - their own image (Genesis 3:1-6). We wanted to be wise. We wanted to be gods. I say "we" because I would have eaten the fruit too. Since the time of Eden, we have built our towers toward heaven in hopes of being gods. We bear our own image in every selfish thought and every selfish deed; perhaps even in every selfie we take. Aren't we long over due to wise up and bear the right image?

As I said before, all our human knowledge is stacked up over many centuries. We build on the ideas of past generations. There is nothing inherently wrong with this. Or is there? I'm a history teacher and I often tell my students to "allow the past to shape the present for the future." This accrued knowledge has the potential to make us wiser, doesn't it? We still desire to be wise, just like Adam and Eve did in the garden. But as image-bearers of ourselves could it be that we seek the wrong type of wisdom?

Before we go on lets define wisdom. Wisdom is good judgment. It is the right application of knowledge and truth. When knowledge is applied rightly, our lives have deeper meaning. There is nothing more meaningful than being image-bearers of the Creator. Unfortunately, even I sometimes wonder if there is something better out there. My perspective is 'bent,' as C.S. Lewis puts it in his science fiction classic, Out of the Silent Planet. My perspective needs to be straightened out. This won't happen while the children of the present seek the knowledge and wisdom of the bent and sinful contributors of the past. This is the wrong sort of wisdom. (I know that elements of truth can be found in any culture. All truth is God's truth no matter where it is found but that is not in the scope of this podcast.) The Bible tells us what the right kind of wisdom is:

Who is wise and understanding among you? By his good conduct let him show his works in the meekness of wisdom. But if you have bitter jealousy and selfish ambition in your hearts, do not boast and be false to the truth. This is not the wisdom that comes down from above, but is earthly, unspiritual, demonic. For where jealousy and selfish ambition exist, there will be disorder and every vile practice.

But the wisdom from above is first pure, then peaceable, gentle, open to reason, full of mercy and good fruits, impartial and sincere. And a harvest of righteousness is sown in peace by those who make peace. (James 3:13-18)

According to this passage there is such a thing as Godly-wisdom. James says that you will know those who are truly wise because they are humble, they are selfless, they are peacemakers. We should look for the right kind of wisdom in the wisest of role models. We should look to Christ - the Son of God - the "last Adam" (1 Cor. 15:45) who bore the image of His Father perfectly and in a way that no other human could before Him by bearing God's image all the way to the cross and beyond. One of the best places to find this Jesus is in the Gospels. The Gospels show us how Jesus lived and loved. I have often wondered why Christ wasn't just sacrificed as a baby. It's conceivable that Herod could have accomplished that task early on. But the Gospel isn't only the death and resurrection of Christ. It is also His life. Jesus had to show us how to bear the image of God rightly. And now He beckons his children to follow him. Matthew 16 says this: "Then Jesus told his disciples, "If anyone would come after me, let him deny himself and take up his cross and follow me. For whoever would save his life will lose it, but whoever loses his life for my sake will find it." (Matt. 16:24-25) Christ calls his disciples to walk in humility by putting Him and everyone else before ourselves. By doing so we can truly be wise as James describes wisdom.

May we grow to be humble, selfless, peacemakers that rightly bear the image of God and fulfill our part in the Maker's grand story of love and redemption.

(End of transcripts)

Loving family always requires selflessness. Most of the time it demands being intentional. My family is a precious gift from God. They are entrusted to me and I to them. My wife and children are my primary ministry, second only to God.

I enjoy my family by communing with them and serving them.

TIPS: A FEW WAYS THAT WE DO LIFE

- I realize that my time is not my own while my family is awake. So I do most of my creative work after my family goes to sleep, unless I have scheduled it in advance.
- I make an effort to stay off of my cell phone at home. Some days are better than others.
- My wife, JoAlison, and I are intentional about family Bible study and prayer. This

normally happens at table and most often at breakfast.

- We all look one another in the eyes when communicating.

- I'm not as animated as I could be so, JoAlison reminds me to smile at our children :)

- My wife and I go on a date every week with the loving aid of our mothers who both babysit our children weekly.

- We spend alone time with each of our four children.

- We play with our children. (I know this should go without saying but I have heard that some parents don't play with their kids.)

- We read to our children several nights a week. We have read at least thirty novels as a family.

- JoAlison and I read to each other (this is one of my favorite things). As a couple, we have read more books than I can count.

- I don't spend a lot of time with my other friends (sorry fellas). I go home so that I have time to do all the above. Again, my time is not my own. It belongs to my family.

FOCUS THREE: COMMUNITY

"Behold, how good and pleasant it is when brothers dwell in unity!" (Psalms 133:1)

I am made for relationship. I am not made to walk alone. A community provides fellowship, love, and accountability. I find joy in my community by doing life with my local church. My joy increases when we, as a body, spread the good news, worship Christ and grow in the knowledge of the Lord, serve one another and our town, hold one another accountable and pray together, and when we eat and play together. Below is another episode of the Ponder This Podcast which deals with this subject.

PONDER THIS: EPISODE ONE

THE MAGIC OF SHARING A MEAL

"If more of us valued food and cheer and song above hoarded gold, it would be a merrier world."
—J.R.R. Tolkien (8)

Thorin Oakenshield was on to something when he spoke these dying words to Bilbo Baggins in The Hobbit. There is something magical about sharing a meal with those that you love—whether it be with family, friends, or community.

From the foragers bringing back their findings to the Agrarians bringing in the harvests, the practice of gathering to share food is something we humans have done since the beginning. What is it about food, on a table, surrounded by people that can produce such childlike mirth within us all?

People loosen up at the table - they get real. In the rush of daily life we are quick to tell our friends that we're doing okay even if we really aren't. But when our community shares a meal together the, "everything is awesome" mask tends to be set aside. The genuine side of person comes out. It is a beautiful thing to behold because when people are honest with one another relationships are strengthened, lives are mended and can be made whole in Christ. It is a part of the process of edification that is only found in fellowship with one another. At table, confession often happens, iron sharpens iron, lives are changed. Nowhere is this more clearly seen than at the end of the second chapter of Acts:

> They devoted themselves to the apostles' teaching and to fellowship, to the breaking of bread and to prayer. Everyone was filled with awe at the

many wonders and signs performed by the apostles. All the believers were together and had everything in common. They sold property and possessions to give to anyone who had a need. Every day they continued to meet together in the temple courts. They broke bread in their homes and ate together with glad and sincere hearts, praising God and enjoying the favor of all the people. And the Lord added to their number daily those who were being saved. (Acts 2:42–47)

Scripture paints this inspiring picture of the early church sharing meals together, daily. From this passage, it would seem that the believer's lifestyle of sharing in Christian-fellowship led to the favor of the community at large. Perhaps the people of Jerusalem (where this particular church was located) saw how sincere, how honest, how loving the Christian family was toward each other? Perhaps this then caused the spectators to want what the Christians had. Whatever the reason for "the people's favor," Luke clearly shows that this close-knit community led people to faith in Christ: "And the Lord added to their number daily those who were being saved." (Acts 2:47)

Daily. Wow!

May we learn the lesson of valuing food and cheer and song more than worldly riches, as Tolkien suggested via a dying dwarf. I am sure that even Thorin Oakenshield saw beyond the food and song to the heart of the matter: mankind sharing in the true riches of life, being loved by God and loving Him and neighbor in return. These are the gifts that have been so freely and abundantly given to us through Christ. It is our ability to share His love with others at table and elsewhere that is the true magic of the world.

(End of transcripts)

FOCUS FOUR: EDUCATION

While this subject has already been touched on as a *Good Winter Offering* there are a few more things I would like to add to the matter as it pertains to my focus on education.

There are two ways to approach education. The first is classic, handed down to us from such teachers as Aristotle. He believed that we learn to enrich our human experience. For instance, we study philosophies of the past to better understand of the people that came before us. In turn, this can help us better understand why we think and act like we do today. The other approach to learning is a more modern one that I imagine you are familiar with. It is the method that says education is a means to an end. For example, we go to college to get the higher paying job. I believe that when we view education like this we are far more likely to forget the things that we 'learned'. How many times have you heard someone say that they remember nothing they learned in school? I can't keep up with the count.

I believe the classic view to be the better one, though I certainly employ the modern method as well. So it might be best to say that a combination of the two is best.

I learn to live a higher quality life and to better understand the gift of life given to me. As knowledge adds value to my life, I, in turn, teach to add value to the lives of others.

Like with the other focuses, this points outward not inward. My education leads to the education of others. I never want to hoard knowledge for myself. This is perhaps seen most clearly in my work. I have pastored a church and taught both middle school and high school for most of my adult life. What ever you do serve God and others.

FOCUS FIVE: STORYTELLING

Telling stories is one of my favorite things to do! A good story has the power to captivate and shift thoughts. A story can be used for noble or twisted purposes. I tell stories for the former reason. I do so through many mediums: teaching, writing, singing, podcasting, and designing. Some of my work is fictitious but even myth can reveal powerful truths about reality. C.S. Lewis says this about myth:

> The value of the myth is that it takes all the things we know and restores to them the rich significance which has been hidden by 'the veil of familiarity.' The child enjoys his cold meat, otherwise dull to him, by pretending it is buffalo, just killed with his own bow and arrow. And the child is wise. The real meat comes back to him more savory for having been dipped in a story...by putting bread, gold, horse, apple, or the

very roads into a myth, we do not retreat from reality: we rediscover it. (9)

The stories I create are designed to kindle wonder. We need wonder in our lives. The Christian must have it. As I've already mentioned, in another chapter, without wonder we cannot fully worship God. A sense of awe toward God must exist to sincerely bow before Him.

I believe that the Lord delights in seeing us fulfill our individual callings. I'm not advocating for you to just go out there and follow your heart. Our hearts are still affected by the fall and they can lead us wrong when we are not seeking first the Kingdom of God. That is not to say that we don't reach for our dreams. But we should take great care that what we are reaching for aligns with God's design. This occurs when we are putting GOD, FAMILY, and COMMUNITY first in our lives.

While I have five major focuses in life some people might have six or maybe even seven. I would caution the reader against pursuing too many things at a time. As I said before, when I focus on more than I should I am frustrated and less productive. I have a practical method of keeping myself in check. If time with the community comes before time with my family I make adjustments. If time with family comes before my time God, I adjust. EDUCATION and STORYTELLING should always come last on my list. If there is time for these focuses then so be it. If not then my priorities are right. This is the key to keeping my focus on the things that matter most. This leads to greater joy.

Obviously, I find joy in each of these focus areas. But I'm not perfect. Sometimes I forget the joy of reading the Bible, especially when I treat it like a textbook. When my kids are arguing with each other and the clamor crescendos, I lose sight of the joy there. And most of the time serving others is just plain messy. People are hurting and in need of a Savior. As we serve our neighbor we will face trials. God will call us to righteousness and self-sacrifice. It will hurt to become more like Christ. Still, we find immense joy when we abide in Jesus. James, the brother of Jesus, says, "Count it all joy, my brothers, when you meet trials of various kinds, for you know that the testing of your faith produces steadfastness. And let steadfastness have its full effect, that you may be perfect and complete, lacking in nothing." (James 1:2-4)

We must seek joy on every occasion, even when we have to dig deep to spot it.

Good Winter
OFFERING FIVE: CLEANSING

Winter undoubtedly purifies the land. It washes it and brings it into a state of hushed dormancy. Winter can have this same effect on us if we let it. When we slow down it is easier to see what really matters. It is also easier to see where we may have been frivolous with our resources. Owning lots of things might be your thing. But if it's not and you'd like to be less distracted by what you own then keep reading.

OWN WHAT ADDS VALUE

It all starts with the concept of value. Few goods and services add lasting value to life. Be content with minimal consumption to make room for what really matters. Remember my email story from the last chapter? It felt great to get rid of 8,000 emails! I didn't need them. I had lost track of what was in that virtual pile. I despised opening my email account. It was a burden on my mind. But once I'd taken the time to remove what was unnecessary and save the things that were, I felt immediate relief. I could see what truly needed attending to.

I am a collector by nature. I've collected coins, posters, records, movies, *nerd alert* Apple products, comic books, Star Wars memorabilia, Nintendo gaming consoles and renaissance festival mugs. Yeah, you read right - renaissance festival mugs. I apologize if you feel you now know me better than you ever wanted to. My most prized collection is books, some dating all the way back to the mid 19th century. I also hold on to things like my children's artwork and articles belonging to parents, grandparents and great-grandparents. I'm too sentimental. It drives my wife crazy sometimes. JoAlison is a minimalist by nature and I'm a wannabe.

It took me a long time to admit that collections can become clutter. At one time I had accrued so much stuff that I no longer knew what I had or where it all was (like that email account). I no longer knew what I valued in my sea of sentimentality. I needed a new mindset. We decided to own only what adds value to our lives. It was time to get rid of one or two things. My wife and I worked together to accomplish this goal for our entire family. We have not arrived yet.

As we began this process we realized that the clutter went beyond my many collections. There was too much stuff everywhere. We've removed thousands of items from our home. Thousands, I tell you! Take a moment to consider how many things you have stuffed here and packed there. It can be over-whelming, right? The sad part is that many of the things we keep we use only once or twice. We know this and yet we don't let go. Why?

There was a time when people were taught not to let go of what they had and for good reasons. There is an elderly woman named

Margaret at the church I pastor. Margaret grew up in England during the Depression Era. She lived just outside of London when the Blitzkrieg occurred. What stories! Anyway, she has told me of her generations desire to hold on to anything that might be useful. This was ingrained in her from an early age because the depression had taken everything from her and her family. Thankfully, we aren't living in the Depression Era any longer. I have walked this earth for nearly four decades and have wanted for very little. This is our blessing in the west, and perhaps our curse. That, however, is topic for another work. In the consumerist-culture that we live in our challenge is staying afloat in a sea of material goods. It's time to drain the waters a little. It is time to let go of what we do not need and it could take longer than the winter months allow for. My wife and I are still shedding weight years after we began this cleansing. But it is has been rewarding to be free of the clutter, knowing that what we have, we really want.

TIPS: WAYS TO DECLUTTER YOUR HOME

- We purged the bookshelves keeping the ones that were like friends. I gave the rest to coworkers.
- We scoured our closets and chests for rarely worn clothes. Keep in mind that we are a family of six so there were tons. These, we gave to family and charities.
- We dug through all the boxes in the attic, consolidating what really mattered and removing the rest.
- We joined local online groups and sold unused furniture, bicycles, rugs, toys etc.
- Then we did it all over again.
- And again.

Afterwards, we realized the most challenging task was still before us. It is relatively easy to remove clutter from your house. The hard part is keeping the stuff out. This requires being conscientious about all future purchases.

At first, my wife and I were good at keeping the newly empty spaces empty. Over time we found ourselves repeating old habits. Like hanging new art on the wall that we purchased on a whim. Window shopping is a dangerous pastime for us. Now we try to go to stores only when we need to.

You don't have to go as crazy with this step like us but for my wife and me, it was an answer to retaining a semblance of sanity in our six-person home.Now if we could just keep the kids on board with our philosophy! Alas, some battles are easier than others.

TO END

Though winter may be bleak, there is much joy and celebration to be derived from winter time. I hope you, good reader, have been left with a bit of inspiration through the things I've shared in this smallish guide. Just to recap, the winter has much to offer if we view things properly - the stars that shine in abundance, the warmth that we create together, the time we have to ponder and learn and to be more perfectly formed. Finally we have a chance to cleanse our homes and minds from the clutter we've accumulated over the course of the previous year. To some, I have, perhaps, stated the obvious. If this is you, I hope you have been reminded of a reason or two to find joy in the cold months. To others, I hope I have kindled a torchlight to warm your winter in new ways. Maybe you will be able to say, along with my family, "Good Winter!"

END NOTES

1. Burns, Robert. "Winter: A Dirge." *Poetry Foundation*, www.poetryfoundation.org/poems/53211/winter-a-dirge. Accessed 28 Dec. 2017.

2. Williams, Sarah. "The Old Astronomer to His Pupil." *Arecibo Observatory*, www.naic.edu/~gibson/poems/swilliams1.html. Accessed 28 Dec. 2017.

3. Esv: Study Bible : English Standard Version. Wheaton, Ill: Crossway Bibles, 2007. Print.

4. "Seven Sisters Get WISE." *NASA*, www.nasa.gov/mission_pages/WISE/multimedia/gallery/pia13121.html. Accessed 28 Dec. 2017.

5. Christoforou, Peter. "Interesting Facts About Orion." *Astronomy Trek*, 25 Nov. 2012, http://www.astronomytrek.com/step-4-interesting-facts-about-orion/. Accessed 28 Dec. 2017.

6. Thoreau, Henry D. Walden or Life In the Woods. Princeton University Press. 2004.

7. McKelvey, Doug. "100-Year Vision." *The Rabbit Room*, 30 May 2016, http://rabbitroom.com/2016/05/100-year-vision/. Accessed 28 Dec. 2017.

8. Tolkien, J.R.R. The Hobbit. Mariner Books, 2012.

9. Lewis, C.S. On Stories: And Other Essays on Literature. Mariner Books. 2002.

ABOUT THE AUTHOR

Dylan Higgins is a pastor, educator, and writer.
He lives with his wife and four children at
Hill Hårow, their home in Georgia.

For more visit hillharow.com